Solid Foundation™ Sermon Starters

BOOK OF ACTS

Blueprints for 30 messages built upon God's Word

Alger Fitch

Cincinnati, Ohio

Cover design by Grannan Graphic Design LTD

Interior design by Robert E. Korth

Edited by Jim Eichenberger

Printed in the U.S.A.

07 06 05 04 03 02 01 00 5 4 3 2 1

Contents

Ingredients for a New Pentecost

Acts 1:1-26

The birthday of the church, like other birthdays, can be remembered but not repeated. However, the healthy growth of the early church can be duplicated wherever these pre-Pentecost ingredients can be found.

I. **"P" IN PENTECOST STANDS FOR "PRAYER" (v. 14).**
Prayer precedes, permeates, and perpetuates all revival.

II. **"E" IN PENTECOST STANDS FOR "EXPECTANCY" (v. 6).**
The apostles lived on tiptoe, expecting something great to happen. They anticipated God was about to intervene.

III. **"N" IN PENTECOST STANDS FOR "NO EXCUSE" (v. 8).**
Twelve men are given the seemingly impossible order of informing city, nation, and world. Instead of making excuses they made good.

IV. **"T" IN PENTECOST STANDS FOR "TEACHING" (v. 3).**
Jesus had taught these men in his ministry before the cross. Now come forty days of "graduate studies" on the kingdom. Bible knowledge is a key element for church growth.

V. **"E" IN PENTECOST STANDS FOR "EXAMPLE" (v. 13).**
Each apostle is listed by Luke as present and accounted for. Can they hardly call others to be faithful, if they themselves are absentees?

VI. **"C" IN PENTECOST STANDS FOR "CONVICTION" (v. 3).**
A "convict" is a man behind bars, making escape difficult, if not impossible. A person of "conviction" cannot run away from facts.

VII. **"O" IN PENTECOST STANDS FOR "ORGANIZATION" (vv. 15-26).**
Half of Acts chapter one is given to the bringing of the apostolic twelve back to its full number. Founded on the memorial day when the twelve tribes had been formed into a theocracy at Sinai, it was vital that the church be seen as the new Israel. This made the number 12 important. Detailed planning and careful organization in our outreach programs is also top priority.

VIII. "S" IN PENTECOST STANDS FOR "SINGLENESS" (v. 14).

If you want a cake like Mama used to bake, you need the ingredients Mama used to use. A basic element in early church evangelism was the "one accord" (KJV) that marked this early band of believers. Unity, harmony, and oneness are words that describe soul-winning at its best.

IX. "T" IN PENTECOST STANDS FOR "TESTIMONY" (ACTS 2–28).

After the opening chapter of Acts that tells of the preparation that preceded the gospel's spread across the world, the witnessing church gets at its assigned task of fulfilling Jesus' Great Commission.

ILLUSTRATION

If in the first century Jesus can take this odd assortment of men and build a church, there is hope for every congregation on earth. One can hardly believe that such common men of various occupations could be of "one accord." Simon the Zealot got his name designation by his intense opposition to Roman domination over the Jews in Palestine. Matthew (Levi) exacted taxes from the Jewish people for the coffers of the invading force. Yet, here they are continuing "constantly in prayer, along with the women and Mary the mother of Jesus, and with his brothers" (v. 14).

Our Church Is Pentecostal!

Acts 2:1-47

Today, the label, "Pentecostal," may bring both positive and negative reactions to a congregation of listeners. Though we often think of the word referring to doctrines of specific denominations, all Christians share certain "Pentecostal" characteristics. Any church will be most pleasing to God and more beneficial to people when it is Pentecostal in the following four ways.

I. OUR CHURCH IS PENTECOSTAL IN ORIGIN (vv. 1-13).

A. The church began on the day of Pentecost.

Pentecost was one of the seven major feast days of God's Old Covenant people. Pentecost, meaning fifty, followed Passover by fifty days and celebrated the giving of the Ten Commandments to Israel. Leviticus 23:14-16 indicates the feast day always fell on a Sunday.

B. The church began by the giving of the Holy Spirit.

On the Pentecost when Israel as a nation was born, the tables of the covenant (the Ten Commandments) were given by God through Moses. In the Acts 2 record, as the Israel of New Covenant days is inaugurated, the Holy Spirit is given by God through Christ. Sin will be overcome not by laws on stone, restraining our actions from without, but by God's Holy Presence producing a righteous fruit from abiding within.

II. OUR CHURCH IS PENTECOSTAL IN MESSAGE (vv. 14-36).

A. Apostolic preaching focused upon the Christ.

The twelve pointed to Jesus, telling of his miracles (v. 22), his cross (v. 23), his resurrection (vv. 24-32), and his ascension and coronation (v. 33).

B. Apostolic preaching announced the gospel.

The good news is the story of Jesus' passion and resurrection (1 Corinthians 15:1-4). Those basic gospel facts are supported by Old Testament Scriptures (vv. 25-28, 34, 35) and apostolic witness (v. 32). The divine promise of salvation through Jesus' sacrifice is the centerpiece of the church's message.

III. OUR CHURCH IS PENTECOSTAL IN LEADING OTHERS TO CHRIST (vv. 37-41).

A. Clear commands were given to those responding to the gospel message.
Peter's inspired proclamation of Jesus as the awaited Messiah caused listeners to respond. When the crowd asked, "Brothers, what shall we do?" (v. 37),Peter answered with the Spirit-given words, "Repent and be baptized" (v. 38). The Bible records their faithful response. "Those who accepted his message were baptized" (v. 41).

B. These commands have been repeated by Christians since that day.
Ten cases of conversion are recorded in the book of Acts. In each case repentance is either mentioned or implied and the decision is sealed with the act of baptism. We are wise to follow that same pattern today.

IV. OUR CHURCH IS PENTECOSTAL IN WORSHIP (vv. 42-47).

A. They assembled for apostolic teaching.
"They devoted themselves to the apostles' teaching" (v. 42). No longer was the guideline for living the Law of Moses. Jesus had opened up the Jewish Scriptures with new insights for his followers. Types had been replaced with eternal realities. Verbal prophecies had found fulfillment in Christ.

B. They assembled for fellowship.
The Greek word koinonia implied sharing together. The old English "fee-lay-ship" suggested each brother and sister brought something (a fee, a talent, a ministry) to benefit others in the body of believers.

C. They assembled for the breaking of bread.
Luke highlights for Theophilus a practice that differentiated Christian gatherings from worship assemblies of other monotheists. Not only did Christians share common meals, they shared a ceremonial meal. In observing the Lord's Supper, the church testified to the death, resurrection, and coming return of their Savior.

D. They assembled for prayer.
The head of the church was once asked by his disciples to teach them to pray (Luke 11:1). This they did privately, in family gatherings, and in full assemblies.

Remove the Asterisk

Acts 2:14-44

It is common for a church hymnal to use an asterisk to mark verses of a song that can be left out without materially affecting the thought being expressed. While such a practice may help churches streamline a service, sometimes important words are left unsung. For example, can we truly make the plea, "Take My Life and Let It Be," without including, "Take my silver and my gold; not a mite would I withhold?"

It is human nature to ignore information and instruction which is difficult or which does not fit into our plans or traditions. When we do so with what the Bible teaches about the message and methods of the early church, we do so at our own risk. Let us look at elements of New Testament preaching and practice and remove any "asterisks" which we may have placed on them.

I. EARLY BELIEVERS PREACHED JESUS' DEATH, BURIAL, AND RESURRECTION (vv. 14-36).

A. Modern theological liberalism places an asterisk on the resurrection of Christ.
According to liberal theology, the physical resurrection of Christ and physical resurrection of believers on the last day are not essential to the faith.

B. The apostle Paul faced a similar problem in the ancient city of Corinth. Paul argued that without a physical resurrection the gospel message is a lie (1 Corinthians 15:15). Furthermore, without a physical resurrection there would be no hope (v. 19). Finally, without a physical resurrection there would be no reason for a bold, mission-minded church (vv. 30-32).

C. We must remove any asterisk we have placed on the physical resurrection of Christ and preach it as confidently as did the early church.

II. EARLY BELIEVERS TAUGHT FAITH, REPENTANCE, AND BAPTISM (vv. 37-41).

A. Faith is a transfer of trust from oneself to God alone.
We place an asterisk adjacent to faith when we define it as simply affirming that God exists. The word translated "faith" is also translated with much stronger-sounding words such as "proof" (Acts 17:31) and "fully trusted" (Titus 2:10). Early believers taught total dependence upon God for salvation.

B. Repentance is a change of allegiance. We commit to meet God's standards rather than our own.

We place an asterisk on repentance today when we fail to stress God's absolute standard of morality. Simply saying, "I'm sorry, God, if I offended you in some small way," and then living as we wish is not how early believers understood repentance.

C. Baptism is a radical act of surrender to God.

When early believers were baptized, they publicly dramatized Christ's saving acts. They physically placed their bodies in the hands of another who "buried" them for a moment in water and "resurrected" them back into a new life (Romans 6:3, 4).

Today we place an asterisk adjacent to baptism if we ritualize it. Baptism in the early church was a choice made by repentant believers. Baptism was a complete immersion in God's grace. A token washing of an infant may have significance in some church traditions, but it misses the impact and testimony of New Testament baptism.

III. EARLY BELIEVERS GATHERED TO STUDY, GIVE, COMMUNE, AND PRAY (vv. 42-44).

A. The early church met to study at the feet of the apostles.

We must never put an asterisk on clear, authoritative, Bible preaching. Only the Word of God can nourish us to fullness in Christ.

B. The early church gave sacrificially.

We must never put an asterisk adjacent to giving. In our selfish culture we must encourage each other to live more simply in order to meet the needs of others.

C. The early church regularly observed the Lord's Supper.

We must never put an asterisk on this most significant meal. In this way we are constantly reminded of our unity as a single family gathered around the table and the price paid for that unity.

D. The early church prayed with fervency.

We must never put an asterisk next to making petition to God. Prayer not programming was the priority of the first believers.

When Lame Men Walk

Acts 3:1-26

The physical miracles by Christ and his followers were but promises of the greatest wonder of all—human redemption. To be "saved" is to be "made whole." Our fallen world is filled with moral cripples, people spiritually blind, young and old too weak to stand erect in the face of temptation. The Bible is a Doctor Book with the cure.

I. ARE YOU A BEGGAR?

A. It is blessed to receive the good news.
A Christian soul-winner has been said to be but one beggar telling another hungry beggar where to find bread.

B. "It is more blessed to give than to receive" (Acts 20:35).
Having received Christ, you should experience the joy of sharing him.

C. It is blessed to be carried (v. 2) and not left behind.

D. It is more blessed to carry others to Jesus.
We are won to win and told to tell.

II. ARE YOU A CRIPPLE?

A. It is sin that cripples us, making us beggars.

B. It is sin that paralyzes us with fear.

C. It is sin that impairs us with hate.

III. ARE YOU WANTING A CURE?

A. Wholeness is in the name of Jesus (v. 6).
There is no other name that can effect our salvation.

B. Wholeness is for the asking at our temple door (v. 2).
While the world looks for completeness in so many activities, there is no need to go anywhere other than to the church of Jesus Christ.

C. Wholeness is given by our outstretched hand (v. 7).
There is no reason you cannot reach another for Christ.

CONCLUSION

Our church door will be known as the "Gate called Beautiful" (v. 10) if we bring the lost through the entrance.

TEXTUAL HIGHLIGHTS

Chapters two and three of Acts both contain sermons and both begin with a miraculous event. It was not first a song service, then an extended sermon, and finally the many miracles of healing and the experience of spiritual outpourings. A careful reading shows the order to be a single wonder to attract the audience followed by the message that explained the gospel.

In the first case (Acts 2) "Jews from every nation under heaven" were hearing "Galileans" speaking in their "own native language." It mattered not from what land they had come or in what dialect they had their origin; these unlearned apostles had the listener's idioms and accents down to perfection. The obvious miracle showed God's approval of the message. Hence, "About three thousand were added to their number that day."

The second miracle recorded (Acts 3) likewise precedes, rather than follows, the message. It was a dramatic occurrence. This man was "crippled from birth" (3:2) and that sad birth was "over forty years" earlier (4:22). It was no feigned healing on an unknown. For all these years pilgrims to the temple had seen the lame man asking alms during each festival, as they entered the temple. They did not just hear a rumor of his healing; they saw him in the temple, "walking and jumping and praising God" (3:8). With such an irrefutable demonstration of Christ's power in their presence, what else could they do but accept the apostle Peter's message (4:4)?

ILLUSTRATION

Qualified to give. Peter has said, "Silver or gold I do not have, but what I have I give you" (v. 6). 1 cannot give you the measles if I do not have the measles. No person can give another the Savior until he has the Savior. If you have Christ, you can give Christ to another. The cripple's first steps brought him into the temple. Let that be true of all the redeemed. When our lives give evidence to the change Christ can bring, many more folks will join us at the worship time.

The Original Sin

Acts 4:32–5:17

Many books on theology use the technical term, "original sin." Today we will use the phrase in a different sense. Luke's first description of an act of evil in the church shows how sin marred the life of the early believers.

I. THE ORIGINAL PURITY IN THE CHURCH (4:32-37)

A. The early church manifested oneness in the midst of diversity. "All the believers were one in heart and mind."

B. The early church manifested generosity in the midst of need. "They shared everything they had."

II. THE ORIGINAL SIN IN THE CHURCH (5:1-4)

A. At the beginning of human history, the sin of Adam and Eve was related to greed. "When the woman saw that the fruit of the tree was good for food and pleasant to the eye, and also desirable for gaining wisdom, she took some and ate it" (Genesis 3:6).

B. At the beginning of church history, the sin of another couple, Ananias and Sapphira, also related to greed. "With his wife's full knowledge he kept back part of the money for himself."

III. THE ORIGINAL PUNISHMENT ON THE CHURCH (5:5-11)

A. Our loving God needed to remind his people that he metes out justice to those who reject grace.

B. Our forgiving God needed to remind his people that he will punish those who refuse to repent.

TEXTUAL HIGHLIGHTS

Does the Bible teach private ownership of property? It is safe to say that the Scripture affirms divine ownership and a call for human stewardship. Luke describes the attitude toward things in the earliest church. He writes, "No one claimed that any of his possessions was his own" (4:32). He tells of brethren willing to sell "lands or houses" so the apostles could distribute "to anyone as he had need" (vv. 34, 35).

Following this happy description comes a specific grand example and one case of betrayal of the sharing spirit. Barnabas is selected to illustrate the general caring attitude, because he will later be a major character in the book as a prominent missionary in the church. The bad example stated has made the names of Ananias and Sapphira infamous throughout church history.

Pretense was the specific sin. Play acting was the temptation. Wanting to appear generous like the others, yet grasping to their goods, they "lied . . . to God" (5:4).

No law forced believers to sell their possessions, but brotherly love stimulated the multitude of the them that believed to want to meet the need of the Christian family in Jerusalem. No communist philosophy said their homes and lots belonged to the church or government. Peter reasoned, "Didn't it belong to you before it was sold? And after it was sold, wasn't the money at your disposal?" (5:4). To this day, benevolent work is supported by the believing community out of sheer voluntary love. To this hour, missionaries are sent to foreign lands and young minds are trained in Christian schools because of a magnificent obsession. Good news is too good to keep to oneself.

ILLUSTRATION

Original sin. In an earlier day, when nightly evangelistic services attracted large crowds, a preacher's advertised topic caught the attention of a man who usually had no time for the church. The flier advertising the revival announced that on Sunday night the subject would be "original sin." The local reprobate was interested, so the story goes, because he so enjoyed his life of sin that he wanted to hear about a novel way to sin he may have overlooked!

A Church With Growing Pains

Acts 6:1-7

Biblical figures of speech for the church recognize the great variety of needs and talents there are in a congregation: body of Christ, temple of God, Kingdom of Heaven, to name a few. The congregation was never intended to be a one-man affair. Each person is needed. Every one has abilities to contribute and needs for others to meet. Teamwork is the solution.

I. THE PROBLEM: THERE WAS TOO MUCH WORK FOR TOO FEW WORKERS (v. 1).

A. The 3,000 of Acts 2:41 had become the 5,000 of Acts 4:4. How could 12 men possibly meet every contingency?

B. Every member has need to be ministered to. Yet every member has need to minister to others.

II. THE QUESTION: WHAT IS A PREACHER'S PRIMARY JOB (v. 2)?

A. Priorities must be determined. Some activities are less important than others (v. 2).

B. Preaching the Word of God and prayer are of the highest priority (v. 4).

III. THE SOLUTION: DIVIDE UP THE WORK (vv. 3-6).

A. Give place to the apostolic recommendations (v. 3).

B. Give prominence to the apostolic requirements (vv. 3, 5).

C. Give preference to the congregation's choice (v. 5).

IV. THE RESULT: VICTORIES CONTINUED (v. 7).

A. Sharing the responsibility was good for the apostles: "the word of God spread."

B. Sharing the responsibility was good for the church: the complaining ceased.

C. Sharing the responsibility was good for the community: "the number of disciples in Jerusalem increased rapidly."

D. Sharing the responsibility was a factor in overcoming theological barriers: "a large number of priests became obedient to the faith."

E. Sharing the responsibility was good for the "deacons": Stephen (Acts 7) and Philip (Acts 8) developed as leaders.

TEXTUAL HIGHLIGHTS

Every church needs deacons. At least they need people who render glad and useful service, as the term "deacon" implies. Stephen and Philip were among the seven chosen. They helped serve (Acts 6:2) immediately and helped preach soon thereafter (Acts 7–8).

The biggest surprise in the sixth chapter of Acts is not that "the number of disciples in Jerusalem increased rapidly." It is not that "a large number of priests became obedient to the faith" (6:7). To me the startling fact is that apostles, with all the authority that went with their office, did not select the needed deacons. They trusted the congregation of Mr. and Mrs. Average Member to make their own choice.

The democracy that had arisen in Greece did not give the vote to every person in the land. The democracy growing up under the influence of Christ allows every churchman's voice to be heard. That will remain true even when the gospel reaches Colossae, and slave-owner (Philemon) and slave (Onesimus) will be equal brothers in the same church. Peter tells the ruffled Jerusalem congregation: "Brothers, choose seven men from among you" (6:3).

The congregation, free to make its selection of workers, is not free to lower the standard of life this ministry expects. The kind of person they are to seek is one who has a good head ("full of wisdom"), a good life ("of good report," ASV) and a good heart ("full of the Spirit").

ILLUSTRATION

Priesthood of all believers. Every Sunday's worship bulletin at Salem, Oregon's First Christian Church has on its masthead, "The members are the ministry." We all need reminding of the clear Bible teaching that each believer is a priest before God—a mediator of Christ's grace to the world. (See 1 Peter 2:9 and Revelation 1:5, 6.)

How to Look Like an Angel

Acts 6:5–7:60

Stephen, one of the seven elected to serve the Jerusalem church, became the first martyr in the cause of Christ. Acts 6 and 7 is the record of this only disciple of Christ whose death is given in detail.

Acts 6:15 is the verdict of the Jewish Sanhedrin that Stephen's "face was like the face of an angel." Faces glow when hearts are full. Then deacons shine like beacons. You, too, can be filled with the Spirit, wisdom, faith, grace, and power.

I. STEPHEN'S DEATH HAS PARALLELS TO JESUS' DEATH.

A. Like Christ, he went through trials (6:12).

B. Like Christ, he faced false accusers (6:13).

C. Like Christ, he was charged with similar crimes (6:11-14).

D. Like Christ, he underwent a transfiguration (6:15).

E. Like Christ, he criticized the Sanhedrin (7:51).

F. Like Christ, he saw God in heavenly glory (7:55, 56).

G. Like Christ, he was taken out of the city (7:58).

H. Like Christ, he was condemned to death (7:58).

I. Like Christ, he committed his spirit to hands beyond his own (7:59).

J. Like Christ, he prayed God's forgiveness on his enemies (7:60).

II. STEPHEN'S LIFE HAS PARALLELS TO JESUS' LIFE.

A. Like Christ, Stephen ministered in grace and power (6:8).

B. Like Christ, Stephen taught in wisdom and Spirit (6:10).

C. Like Christ, Stephen manifested faith and character (6:5).

CONCLUSION

One must live like Jesus if he or she would die like him. To die successfully, imitating the Savior is the result of the sufficient cause of living daily in his way and work.

TEXTUAL HIGHLIGHTS

Many are the Bible passages that visualize God seated on the throne of the universe. Peter advocated from the first day of the church that Jesus was now seated on Heaven's throne with the Father. He quoted David's prediction about that relationship from Psalm 110:1: "The Lord said to my Lord: 'Sit at my right hand until I make your enemies a footstool for your feet'" (Acts 2:34, 35). Yet, as Stephen the first Christian martyr faces stoning before the angry mob, he looks toward Heaven and beholds an unusual scene. Amid the glory of God, Jesus is "standing at the right hand of God" (7:55, 56).

Sitting enthroned symbolizes reigning over the church and the cosmos. Standing pictures concern over what is happening. What is done to the least of Christ's brethren matters to Christ (Matthew 25:45). He rises to receive his servant home.

ILLUSTRATION

What's inside? Imagine a person running down the aisle of a crowded sports arena carrying a full bucket or pail. An unkind fan sticks out his leg and trips the runner, causing him to fall and spill the contents in his pail. What will spill out onto the aisle? Will it be water? or sand? or milk? or confetti? The certain answer has to be "Whatever was in the bucket at that time!" When Stephen faced his martyrdom, as the first Christian to give his life in the cause of Jesus, what came out of him was the Christ with whom he had filled his life. Luke tells us he was "full of the Spirit," full of "wisdom" (6:5), full of "grace" (6:8), and full of "power" (6:8). This is another way of saying his life was overflowing with Jesus.

Can the Living Communicate With the Dead?

Acts 8:1-25

For lost and searching people, the occult often holds appeal. People seek special wisdom from beyond themselves, secrets from the spirit world, especially from those from this world who have gone on to the next.

The Bible, however, expressly forbids communication with the dead (Deuteronomy 18:14-15; 1 Chronicles 10:13, 14; Isaiah 8:19, 20; Luke 16:30, 31). This ban is not in place because God desires to keep useful information from us. Rather, he desires that we not be distracted from the only supernatural source of true wisdom and strength (2 Timothy 3:16, 17; John 16:13; Jude 3).

On the other hand, this same Bible calls on us to speak to the spiritually dead. This passage of Scripture reveals important themes concerning reaching out to those separated from the Source of Life.

I. CONSIDER THE MORTALITY OF LOST SINNERS (EPHESIANS 2:1; 1 TIMOTHY 5:6; REVELATION 3:1; LUKE 15:24; ROMANS 6:23; 5:12).

A. Outside of Christ, Saul (the persecutor) had no hope (Acts 8:1).

B. Outside of Christ, Samaritans (the Jews who had intermarried with pagan peoples) had no hope (vv. 1-4).

C. Outside of Christ, Simon (the sorcerer) had no hope (v. 9-11).

II. CONSIDER THE MESSAGE OF LIFE IN CHRIST.

A. Christ was the message heard by Saul (v. 1).

B. Christ was the message heard in Samaria (vv. 4, 5).

C. Christ was the message heard by Simon (vv. 12, 13).

III. CONSIDER THE MEDIUMS ARE LOVING CHRISTIANS (ROMANS 10:15-17).

A. God uses believers' lips to tell His message (vv. 3-6).

B. God uses believers' hands to baptize his converts (vv. 12, 13, 16).

C. God uses believers' prayers to pull back the straying (vv. 18-24).

CONCLUSION

We are alive in Christ. We must communicate with the dead. We have no control over their response. Paul reacted with anger and vengeance after hearing the message of Stephen. Simon the Sorcerer heard the message and slipped back into sinful practice. The Samaritans listened and responded with great joy.

ILLUSTRATION

When were you called? Many years ago as a student preacher I was eating a meal in a member's home after a Sunday morning service. Around the table many questions were asked in the conversation accompanying the meal. One direct inquiry to me that gave me pause was the question, "When did you receive from God your call to preach?"

The question caught me off guard. If I had been asked when I accepted Christ and was baptized, I would have had an immediate and certain response as to day and place. But I could not pinpoint a time at which I was called to ministry. Bible study had just led me to an awareness that all Christians are to share their faith in every way their talents allow. The early Christians demonstrated that same awareness.

No Mirage in the Desert

Acts 8:26-40

We have all heard that when one is in extreme desert conditions, the line between fantasy and reality may blur. One begins to see mirages, images without substance. For the sake of his survival, the desert traveler must be able to distinguish reality from mirages.

As we study Scripture, we too must separate reality from mirages. In the story of Philip and the Ethiopian eunuch, we find four truths about evangelism that are no mirages.

I. IT IS NO MIRAGE THAT GOD DIRECTS THE PROCESS OF EVANGELISM (vv. 26-29).

A. God sent an angel to guide Philip to the right road.

B. God sent the Spirit to guide Philip to the right chariot.

C. God arranged the exact timing in his providence.
The eunuch was traveling east to west; Philip was moving from north to south. Providence caused them to intersect at the exact time.

II. IT IS NO MIRAGE THAT GOD USES WILLING SERVANTS TO PREACH THE GOSPEL (vv. 26-30).

A. Philip could have hesitated, not knowing the destination (v. 26).

B. Philip could have hesitated, fearing a deserted road (v. 26).

C. Philip could have hesitated, feeling inferior to a queen's treasurer (v. 27).

D. Philip could have hesitated, being prejudiced toward an Ethiopian (v. 27).

E. Philip could have hesitated, sensing timidity (vv. 28-30). Rather, he "ran up to the chariot" in swift obedience.

III. IT IS NO MIRAGE THAT THE OLD TESTAMENT REVEALS THE MESSIAH (vv. 30-35).

A. Jesus had taught that he was the fulfillment of Old Testament prophecy (John 5:39; Luke 4:14-21; 24:44).

B. The sermons of the apostles established Jesus' identity as Messiah by quoting the Old Testament (Acts 2:25-35; 3:18-25).

C. Philip the evangelist repeats that same practice (8:30-35).

IV. IT IS NO MIRAGE THAT GOD REACHES OUT TO ALL PEOPLE WITHOUT BIAS.

A. Jesus, in his earthly ministry, welcomed contact with all, including Nicodemus, a member of the Jewish ruling council (John 3:1), an apparently amoral Samaritan woman (John 4:7), and a pious aristocrat (Matthew 19:16), among others.

B. The Ethiopian eunuch differed from Philip racially and was separated from full fellowship in Judaism sexually (Deuteronomy 23:1).

C. Despite these differences, Philip required neither more or less of the Ethiopian than had been required of any others coming to salvation. His conversion shared the same elements of others described previously, including an acceptance of Jesus as the Messiah and baptism (vv. 36-38).

ILLUSTRATION

Christ in the Old Testament. Earlier in United States history when the Bible was regularly read in the classrooms of the public school, some Christian students suggested that only Old Testament passages be read in their school. This suggestion was made because many of their classmates were Jewish. One day, when the reading of Isaiah 53 was given, a murmur was heard.

"They read about the crucifixion and death of Jesus," some insisted. Was the agreement to read only from Old Testament portions of the Bible being violated?

There can be little doubt that the eighth-century prophet Isaiah was talking about Jesus seven hundred years before Jesus was born. Prophecy is history written ahead of time!

The Church of Jesus Christ of Early Day Saints

Acts 8:26-40

Those outside of Christ often greet our efforts to share the gospel with a familiar excuse. "How can I believe what you say," they may argue, "when other so-called Christians believe something totally different?"

This comment has some sad truth to it. Stressing novel and sectarian doctrine causes confusion and division. Christian unity, on the other hand, is enhanced when we emphasize the truths that have been accepted throughout the history of the church. In this passage we see universal truths accepted by the Church of Jesus Christ of Early Day Saints.

I. THE EARLY SAINTS USED A UNIVERSALLY ACCEPTED SCRIPTURE (vv. 32, 33).

A. Philip could have referred to a variety of written religious texts such as the Talmud (written tradition interpreting the Law of Moses) or the writings of currently popular rabbinical schools.

B. Philip, however, began with the universally-received prophecies of Isaiah.

C. A variety of written religious texts exist today, such as the *Book of Mormon* and *Science and Health with a Key to the Scriptures.*

D. Following the example of Philip, we should hold no other book as authoritative other than the Bible.

II. THE EARLY SAINTS PREACHED A UNIVERSALLY ACCEPTED MESSAGE (v. 35).

A. Philip did talk about the works of the apostles or the success of the church in Jerusalem.

B. Philip began with the words of Isaiah and proclaimed the good news of salvation through Jesus.

C. Our mission is not to promote Protestantism, Catholicism, or any other denomination, congregation, or leader. Our message, like Philip's, should be the good news of salvation through Jesus.

III. THE EARLY SAINTS UPHELD UNIVERSALLY-ACCEPTED STANDARDS FOR JOINING THEM (vv. 36-39).

A. Philip did not require the eunuch to meet some standard of knowledge or performance before accepting him as a brother in Christ.

B. The eunuch accepted Philip's argument of Jesus as the promised Messiah and identified with Jesus' death and resurrection by being "buried and raised up" in the act of baptism.

C. Historic creeds and confessions, such as the Nicene Creed, the Chalcedonian Confession, the Apostles' Creed, the Westminster Confession, and so many others have attempted to summarize the beliefs of the church. No lengthy theological study was necessary, however, before the eunuch had the opportunity to accept Jesus.

D. Today we can follow the pattern of Philip and the early church when we accept an adult believer's confession of faith and his baptism as the sole requirements for coming to Christ.

ILLUSTRATION

A confusing process. The husband sought to be helpful to his wife plagued by fever and nausea. He volunteered to prepare her some tea and bring it to her bedside. The rattle of dishes in the kitchen made clear to the wife her mate was having trouble. "Where is the tea?" he called out. "It is as plain as day, if you'll just open your eyes," she responded. "The tea is behind the cupboard door, to the rear of the dishes, in the cocoa tin marked matches!"

Has division in the church made the process of coming to Christ a confusing maze of hidden meanings and secret labels? A confusing multiplicity of sectarian practices and jargon makes the finding of the "one Lord, one faith and one baptism" (Ephesians 4:5) extremely difficult.

Facts Stranger Than Fiction

Acts 9:32-43

It is not unusual for Christians to be asked, "Why do you believe the Bible is true? How do you know that the stories are not simply made up?"

One answer is that the stories the Bible tells are quite different than those one would invent for a religious book. In this section of Scripture, let us examine some typical religious mythology and compare it to the stark realism of God's Word.

I. REGARDING PETER, A LEADER IN THE CHURCH (v. 32)

A. Religious Myth: The "imperial" ruler

1. Wouldn't one expect the church to have a leader who protected his seat of power in an important city? Wouldn't one expect him to spend his time making decrees and decisions and perhaps making plans to hand his power to a successor?
2. Such mythology has become a part of some church traditions which see Peter as the first Pope, a position handed down from generation to generation.

B. Biblical Fact: The servant leader

1. Peter "traveled about the country" rather than ruling from Jerusalem or Rome.
2. Peter visited small and obscure towns to serve in the name of Jesus.

II. REGARDING SAINTS, THOSE MADE HOLY BY GOD (v. 32)

A. Religious Myth: The pious "elite"

1. Wouldn't one expect that church members would have to meet special standards or do extraordinary work to be called "saints"?
2. Some church traditions select a certain group of people to be labeled saints.

B. Biblical Fact: All believers sanctified by grace

1. The Bible refers to all Christians as "saints."
2. There is no class of "super-believers" who have earned holiness by special works. We are made "holy ones" ("saints") by Jesus' work on the cross.

III. REGARDING MIRACLES, GOD'S POWER IN THE CHURCH (vv. 33-42)

A. Religious Myth: Wouldn't one expect miracles to be rewards, given to bring joy and prosperity to those who have the most faith?

B. Biblical Fact: Christ empowered his apostles to perform miracles to authenticate the gospel message, bringing people to faith (vv. 35, 42).

IV. REGARDING MINISTERS, GOD'S SERVANTS IN THE CHURCH (vv. 36-39)

A. Religious Myth: Wouldn't one expect the ministers in the church to be a special class ("clergy"), separated from common members ("laity") by training and special knowledge?

B. Biblical Fact: Every member is a priest and minister (1 Peter 2:9; Revelation 1:6). Dorcas had no special training or ordination, yet she faithfully ministered to the needs of those in Joppa.

TEXTUAL HIGHLIGHTS

Luke hinted at his scheme for Acts in its first chapter. He would tell of the apostles' witness first "in Jerusalem," then "in all Judea and Samaria," and finally "to the ends of the earth" (1:8). He reached his first goal at 6:7, reporting that "the number of disciples in Jerusalem increased rapidly." By 9:31 his second objective was obtained. He pens, "then the church throughout Judea, Galilee and Samaria enjoyed a time of peace." His final target is to show how Christianity flooded into the Gentile world.

This points to the verses that intervene between the second summary verse (9:31) and the opening account of the Gentile thrust, as transition. If Peter is going to open kingdom doors to Cornelius's household in Caesarea, as he did for Jews in Jerusalem, how will he get from one city to the other? Acts 9:32-43 answers the question. Working backward, we read of Cornelius being instructed that he will find Simon in "Joppa" (10:5). The preceding paragraph tells of his ministering there to Dorcas (9:36-43). The prior paragraph tells of Peter's work in Lydda where he received the Joppa call (9:38).

ILLUSTRATION

Every member a minister. One preacher of a large congregation was joking with a proclaimer of the Word from a moderately-sized church. He said, "I'll trade you 500 of my members for 50 of yours. I have only one stipulation. I get to choose both groups." Everyone knows that often the work of the church, like the financial support of the body, is done by a small section of the membership. A Dorcas, putting her sewing skills to work for Jesus, can win respect for the church in its community (v. 39), above the mere presence of "Sunday only" attenders.

I Believe in Miracles

Acts 10:1-48

Oregon's Carlton Buck, a personal friend and long-time minister of Eugene's First Christian Church, wrote:

"I believe in miracles, I've seen a soul set free.
Miraculous the change in life, redeemed at Calvary.
I've seen a lily push its way up through the summer sod.
I believe in miracles for I believe in God."

This inspiring gospel song reminds me of the life-changing conversions that marked Carlton's ministry. Acts 10 deals with life-changing and history-changing conversions. As we study this chapter, let us note three miraculous, divine interventions in evidence there.

I. IT TOOK A MIRACLE TO CONVINCE THE PREACHER THAT HE SHOULD PREACH TO GENTILES.

A. Peter's vision was that the distinction in meats is gone (Acts 10:9-16; Mark 7:19; Romans 14:2, 17; 1 Corinthians 10:23; Colossians 2:16; 1 Timothy 4:3-5).

B. Peter's vision was that the distinction in men is gone (Acts 10:17-36; Galatians 3:28).

II. IT TOOK A MIRACLE TO CONVINCE THE CHURCH THAT THEY SHOULD BAPTIZE GENTILES.

A. The baptism of the Spirit on Cornelius's household was not to save them; the message did that (Acts 11:14).

B. The baptism of the Spirit on Cornelius's household was not to purify their hearts; the faith did that (Acts 15:9).

C. The baptism of the Spirit on Cornelius's household was not to give them faith; hearing the gospel did that (Acts 15:7).

D. The baptism of the Spirit on Cornelius's household was to convince the Jewish Christians to baptize Gentiles into the body (Acts 10:44-48).

III. MAY IT NOT TAKE A MIRACLE TO CONVINCE YOU THAT ALL MEN ARE SAVED THE SAME WAY.

A. Hearing of Christ was needed both then and now (Acts 11:14).

B. Believing in Christ was needed both then and now (Acts 10:43).

C. Repenting toward Christ was needed both then and now (Acts 11:18).

D. Being baptized into Christ was needed both then and now (Acts 10:47, 48).

ILLUSTRATION

Miracles. Miracles are called "wonders" because of the effect they have on observers. They are termed "powers," for they could not happen without divine intervention. The title "signs" signifies they point to a critical truth. We should be careful not to misspeak and use the word "miracle" for every act of God. Jesus himself knew answers to his prayers for many years before turning the water to wine at Cana, which the Bible calls "the first of his miraculous signs" (John 2:11). It was declared that "John [the Baptist] never performed a miraculous sign" (John 10:41). It would be another matter to say he never experienced an answer to his prayers.

The Conversion of the World's Most Moral Lost Man

Acts 10:1, 2, 22; 11:14

The account of the conversion of Cornelius and his household is significant for two reasons. True, this account is significant because it reveals that Gentiles can be converted. But it is also of great significance because it reveals that even the most moral of human beings must be saved by faith in Jesus.

I. **HIS POSITION DID NOT SAVE HIM (10:1).**
"Cornelius, a centurion in . . . the Italian Regiment"

II. **HIS DEVOTION DID NOT SAVE HIM (10:2).**
"He . . . [was] devout."

III. **HIS CREED DID NOT SAVE HIM (10:2).**
"He . . . [was] God-fearing."

IV. **HIS EXAMPLE DID NOT SAVE HIM (10:2).**
"He and all his family"

V. **HIS GENEROSITY DID NOT SAVE HIM (10:2).**
"He gave generously to those in need."

VI. **HIS PRAYERS DID NOT SAVE HIM (10:2).**
"He . . . prayed to God regularly."

VII. **HIS RIGHTEOUSNESS DID NOT SAVE HIM (10:22).**
"He is a righteous . . . man."

VIII. **HIS REPUTATION DID NOT SAVE HIM (10:22).**
"He . . . is respected by all the Jewish people."

IX. **HIS HEEDING THE GOSPEL SAVED HIM (11:14).**
"He [Peter] will bring you a message through which you . . . will be saved."

TEXTUAL HIGHLIGHTS

It was "about noon" (Acts 10:9). That is lunch time. Peter was "on the roof." The ascending aroma of any foods being prepared below would have been reaching the nostrils of the hungry man. Being in Caesarea beside the Mediterranean Sea, the view from the housetop would have included boats moved along by unfurled sails catching the gentle winds. Perhaps those sails, the power by which one traveled to the outermost parts of the earth, was being referred to by the "great sheet, let down by four corners" (10:11). Peter hungered to eat, but the food before him in the vision was unclean. He longed for the satisfaction of telling of the Savior to all people of the world, but his culture considered non-Jews beyond the pale of grace.

The voice calling him to dine was not coming from the evil one, but from the Lord. It was God's only Son who had advocated spreading the gospel "to the whole creation" (Mark 16:15) and discipling "all the nations" (Matthew 28:19). Yet, it was not the way Peter was brought up. God's clear voice had to repeat three times the order, "Get up, Peter. Kill and eat," to overcome the past restrictions that haunted him. Finally the lesson was learned: "God is no respecter of persons" (10:34).

Christians First, Last, and Always

Acts 11:19-30

The prophet Isaiah predicted that God's people would be given "a new name that the mouth of the Lord will bestow" (Isaiah 62:2). When the church moved out of the Jewish world "into all the world," they began being known by that new name. In Antioch, the disciples of Jesus were first called "Christians," meaning "those belonging to the Messiah." That identification with the Savior was a name that fit for a number of reasons.

I. THE NAME FIT, FOR THEY WERE MISSIONARY IN SPIRIT (v. 19).
"telling the message"

II. THE NAME FIT, FOR THEY WERE INCLUSIVE (v. 20).
"began to speak to Greeks also"

III. THE NAME FIT, FOR THEY WERE CHRIST-CENTERED (v. 20).
"telling them the good news about the Lord Jesus"

IV. THE NAME FIT, FOR THEY WERE VISIBLY DIFFERENT (v. 23).
"He . . . saw the evidence of the grace of God."

V. THE NAME FIT, FOR THEY WERE EVANGELISTIC (v. 24).
"And a great number of people were brought to the Lord."

VI. THE NAME FIT, FOR THEY WERE BENEVOLENT (v. 29).
"The disciples . . . decided to provide help for the brothers."

TEXTUAL HIGHLIGHTS

Calling names is not always an evil practice. Two examples of complimentary name-calling are brought to mind as we read Acts 11:19-30. Take the name "Barnabas" in verse 22. We met that name first when Luke was describing the generous "believers . . . of one heart and mind" (4:32) that marked the early Jerusalem congregation. One such unselfish person was Joseph. He gladly sold a field and gave the proceeds to the needy through the apostles. They gave him the surname "Barnabas" (Acts 4:36). It means "Son of Encouragement."

Everywhere we meet Barnabas on the pages of the New Testament, we see how well the nickname fit. Acts 11 describes his pleasure that the gospel was being preached to "Greeks also" (v. 20). Living up to his name, "he encouraged them all to remain true to the Lord with all their hearts" (v. 23). Measuring up to expectation, he seeks out Saul to help in this mission (v. 25). Together they will be counted among the "prophets and teachers" (13:1) of that congregation and later serve side-by-side on the mission thrust into Cyprus and Galatia.

The second sample of name-calling in Acts 11 is at verse 26. "The disciples were called Christians at Antioch." The word Christian is patronymic. That is, it calls to mind "Christ." The letter "i" is a connective and the letters "an" make it a genitive of possession. Hence a Christian is one who belongs to Christ. While some interpreters think the name was hurled in derision by enemies, others believe it to be divinely given by God.

ILLUSTRATIONS

Luther on the name. "I pray you leave my name alone and do not call yourselves Lutherans but Christians."

Wesley on the name. "I would to God that all party names and unscriptural phrases and forms which have divided the Christian world were forgot."

Believe It or Not!

Acts 12:1-25

Ripley's "Believe It or Not" columns in the newspapers have delighted readers for decades with facts that are strange but true. In Acts 12 we are introduced to some facts that would astound even Mr. Ripley!

I. BELIEVE IT OR NOT—ANGELS ARE TOUGH! (vv. 7-11).

A. We sing, "soft as the voice of an angel," in a famous old hymn. Our Christmas trees are decorated with delicate strands of "angel hair." We picture angels as gentle, peaceful, and even feminine beings.

B. Angels in Scripture are quite different. Peter was "struck on the side" and ordered, "Quick, get up!" by a strong, assertive messenger of God. Nothing soft here!

II. BELIEVE IT OR NOT—EVEN FAITHFUL CHRISTIANS MAY SUFFER EXTREME HARDSHIP (vv. 1-4).

A. We think it strange that bad things should happen to good people. Somehow we believe that those who are faithful to God should have trouble-free lives.

B. Luke had already recorded the stoning of Stephen (Acts 7:54-60). History tells us that years later Peter was crucified and Paul was beheaded. In Acts 12, Herod had James "put to death with the sword" (v. 2). Bad things happen, even to God's chosen.

III. BELIEVE IT OR NOT—PRAYER IS POWERFUL (vv. 5, 12).

A. We sometimes minimize prayer. We say, "All we can do now is pray," as though we wished we could do something more effective!

B. This attitude is nothing new. Even though "the church was earnestly praying" for Peter (v. 5), "they were astonished" when the prayers were answered (v. 16)!

IV. BELIEVE IT OR NOT—GOVERNMENT IS NO THREAT TO THE CHURCH (vv. 20-24).

A. While Christians should be salt and light in the world, it is easy to be deceived into believing that political power alone will help the church.

B. This chapter begins with a representative of the most powerful government in the world using his position to attack the church. The chapter ends with his plans foiled and his own life taken from him.

TEXTUAL HIGHLIGHTS

The Bible is known as the book with answers to life's questions. Yet, sometimes as we read it, we find ourselves facing questions for which we cannot find an easy answer. Take Acts 12.

Here we read the exciting story of God's miraculous intervention. Peter is liberated from prison by an angel. His rescue is attributed to the fact that "the church was earnestly praying to God for him" (12:5). Our minds are satisfied. A caring Father lets no Herod keep truth from prevailing. Lights shine in the cell. Chains fall off hands. An iron gate swings open wide (v. 10).

But wait a moment. There is another incident in this chapter. It has to do with John's brother James. The king in afflicting "some who belonged to the church . . . had James put to death" (vv. 1, 2). Does prayer have power only on alternate days? Do some apostles merit protection and others deserve it not? Is a son of Zebedee of less value than "a son of Jonah" (Matthew 16:17)?

We are confident, as the song goes, "we'll understand it better by and by." Even the praying believers in "the house of Mary the mother of John" were surprised when Peter knocked at the door. Why would God allow the death of one apostle and rescue another? They were praying for Peter's boldness and loyalty. They were seeking God's will, not assuming it.

ILLUSTRATION

Temporary empires. Who would have dreamt that the mighty Rome of Julius Caesar, Nero, Domitian, and Diocletian would be outlived by the persecuted church? Who would have imagined that praying Russian peasants would defeat the Communist military by prayers of faith and lives of love? Yet the church lives on, despite the iron fist of ancient Rome and the iron curtain of twentieth-century Communism.

Missionaries That Cannot Fail

Acts 13:1-12

Missionary work is teeming with difficulty. Communicating in an alien culture to those who speak a different language poses unique problems. How can failure be avoided and victory enhanced on the mission field?

The secrets of Paul's success in his missionary endeavors across the world can be discovered in today's text.

I. PAUL HAD EXPERIENCE BENEATH HIM (v. 1).

At this point in his life, Paul was no "greenhorn." He had preached in Damascus, Syria (Acts 9:20-22), Arabia (Galatians 1:17, 18), Tarsus, Cilicia (Acts 11:25), and in Antioch of Syria (Acts 11:26; 13:1). He had some opportunity for "seasoning" before leaving on his first missionary journey.

II. PAUL HAD A FRIEND BESIDE HIM (v. 2).

As Jesus sent early disciples out two-by-two, the Holy Spirit teams together Barnabas and Saul. Two teamed together are always better than one alone (Ecclesiastes 4:9-12).

III. PAUL HAD A CHURCH BEHIND HIM (v. 3).

Laying on of hands by a congregation symbolizes the missionary is not self-sent. He is assured of the financial support, prayer backing, and morale boosting from every member.

IV. PAUL HAD GOD ABOUT HIM (v. 4).

The Holy Spirit was in Paul, went before him, dwelt within him, walked beside him, stood behind him. Whatever the preposition, the Commission-giver surrounds those who carry out his work.

V. PAUL HAD THE WORD WITHIN HIM (v. 5).

He "proclaimed the word of God." Paul was saturated with the message of the gospel, sharing it freely wherever he traveled.

VI. PAUL HAD AN OPPORTUNITY BEFORE HIM (vv. 6-12).

Paul ventured into a world that had never heard the gospel. Starting in Cyprus, he then traveled to Galatia. Within years, due to his influence, the message would reach the darkest corners of the Roman world.

TEXTUAL HIGHLIGHTS

In his homily in the synagogue of Antioch of Pisidia, Paul retells the proud story of Jewish history. Building upon his hearers' love of their roots, Paul describes how God's hand directed their nation's affairs. All the past was a gift from God. Now has come the greatest gift God ever offered Israel. Let the people know that "God has brought to Israel the Savior Jesus" (v. 23).

ILLUSTRATION

Importance of sending missionaries. In several church buildings I have stood before portraits of preachers who had served that body of believers in former years. The years of service with the beginning and closing date of that minister's tenure accompanied each photo and name.

As important as it is to give honor to those who have proclaimed the gospel *in* a specific place, I often wonder about photos I have never seen. How many gospel proclaimers have been sent *from* that place? How many missionaries have been nurtured by that congregation and sent into the needy places of the earth?

Strengthening the Churches

Acts 14:19-28

After his expulsion from Antioch (13:50), being threatened in Iconium (14:2), and having been stoned and left for dead in Lystra (14:19), Paul's reaction may seem strange. Some may have avoided places in which they had bad experiences. Some may have returned, hoping to find a sympathetic shoulder on which to cry. Paul did neither. He returned to each city, not to receive pity, but to give strength to his converts (14:22)!

In these verses we see elements that strengthen churches.

I. EVERY CHURCH IS THE STRONGER WHEN THERE IS EVANGELIZING (v. 21).

A. "They preached the good news in that city."

B. The gospel is God's power to save (Romans 1:16).

II. EVERY CHURCH IS THE STRONGER WHEN THERE IS SOUL-WINNING (v. 21).

A. "They . . . won a large number of disciples."

B. As Jesus said, you "make disciples . . . baptizing them" (Matthew 28:19).

C. Witnessing conversions and the drama of baptism constantly affirms the church in its task.

III. EVERY CHURCH IS THE STRONGER WHEN THERE IS TRAINING (v. 22).

A. "encouraging them to remain true to the faith"

B. As Jesus said, after baptizing should come "teaching them to obey everything . . . commanded" (Matthew 28:20).

IV. EVERY CHURCH IS THE STRONGER WHEN THERE IS ORGANIZING (v. 23).

A. "Paul and Barnabas appointed elders for them in each church."

B. Efficient stores have managers, successful teams have coaches, developing congregations have overseers.

V. EVERY CHURCH IS THE STRONGER WHEN THERE IS UTILIZING (v. 27).

A. "reported all that God had done through them"

B. Paul was a spokesman, Barnabas an encourager, Antioch's members were prayer warriors, letter writers, financial backers, etc.

TEXTUAL HIGHLIGHTS

Three surprises are in the chapter before us. We see the fickleness of man, the tribulations of the righteous, and the essentiality of church elders.

The first surprise is not that there is glad acceptance by some and hateful rejection by others. What appears strange here is that these opposite responses are coming from the same lips. At one moment the preachers are acclaimed to be "gods" (vv. 11, 12). A few lines later the same multitude "stoned Paul" (v. 19). Adam's sons are fickle.

It may also seem strange that "the kingdom of God" and "many hardships" would be joined together in the same sentence. Paul has learned early that "through many hardships" we "enter the kingdom of God" (14:22). Jesus had leveled with his disciples warning, "In this world you will have trouble" (John 16:33). Earth is the battleground for the war of right and wrong. In New Testament times Jesus' followers were not good insurance risks. Surprised?

I am surprised in reading verse 23 that there had been genuine churches of Christ where there had been no elders. Conclusion—Elders are essential to the well-being of the church but not its being.

ILLUSTRATION

How is God using you? Jesus' parables are brief stories with gigantic lessons. He tells of a man going away for awhile, but leaving "his house in charge of his servants, each with his assigned task" (Mark 13:34). Each of us needs to know and carry out "his assigned task." Have you discovered and are you carrying out your particular assignment until Christ returns?

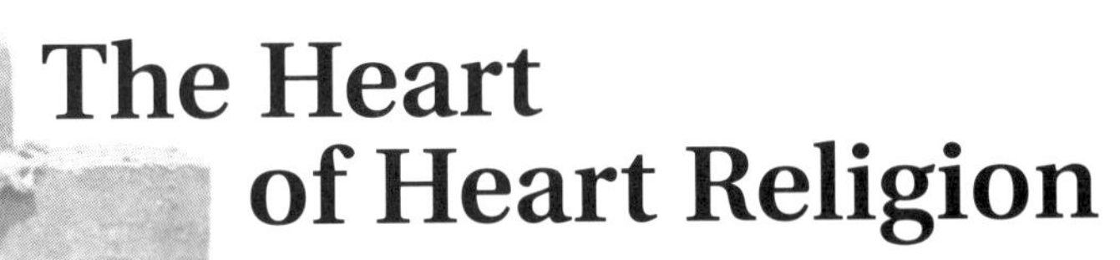

The Heart of Heart Religion

Acts 16:6-15

A word that we use often, but with little understanding, is the word "heart." We use it to describe a simple figure of symmetrical curves that symbolizes love. We use it to describe the durable, muscular pump that faithfully sustains each of our lives. But when the word is used as it is in this chapter, when Lydia "opened her heart to respond to Paul's message" (v. 14), it seems like neither meaning is implied. Let us look more closely at this chapter and get to the heart of the religion of the heart.

I. THE HEART OF GOD SEEKS TO SAVE ALL (vv. 6-13).

A. Even though the Philippians were not seeking God, God was seeking Philippians.

B. Gospel success in Galatia might (with a special call to Macedonia) have led Paul to expect great crowds awaiting. Only a small group of women with neither a man nor a synagogue were waiting. The heart of God sees significance in a group others may count as insignificant.

II. THE HEART OF THE CONVERT IS TOUCHED IN A VARIETY OF WAYS BY THE GOSPEL MESSAGE (v. 14).

A. As the human heart has four chambers, the Bible word "heart" includes four entities.

B. Heart in the Scripture may refer to the intellect.

1. It is said to "think" (Genesis 8:21, KJV; Proverbs 23:7, KJV; Mark 2:8; Acts 8:22).
2. The heart is said to "ponder" (Luke 2:19).
3. The heart is said to "understand" (Matthew 13:15).
4. The heart is said to "meditate" (Psalm 19:14).

C. Heart in the Scripture may refer to the emotions (Matthew 22:37; 6:21; Proverbs 17:22).

D. Heart in the Scripture may refer to the will (Daniel 1:8, KJV; 2 Corinthians 9:7).

E. Heart in the Scripture may refer to the conscience (1 John 3:21; Acts 2:37).

III. THE HEART OF THE GOSPEL IS RADICAL RENEWAL OF A PERSON (vv. 14, 15).

A. Faith indicates a changed mind. "If you believe with all your heart" (Acts 8:37).

B. Repentance indicates changed emotions. "Godly sorrow brings repentance" (2 Corinthians 7:10).

C. Confession indicates a changed will. "If you confess with your mouth . . . and believe in your heart" (Romans 10:9)

D. Baptism brings a changed conscience. "This water symbolizes baptism that now saves you . . . the pledge of a good conscience" (1 Peter 3:21).

CONCLUSION

The key used by God to open the heart is "the Word" (Luke 8:11; Romans 10:17; John 20:30, 31; 17:21).

TEXTUAL HIGHLIGHTS

Luke's material on the expansion of the church is interspersed with announcements of victory. A passage such as Acts 16:5 is called a summary verse. The good news is that "churches were strengthened in the faith and grew daily in numbers."

No one could ask for better results than that. There was growth in conviction and in converts. The numbers kept rising and the quality of faith kept increasing. It is not enough today when some so emphasize the nurture of the saints that they neglect the evangelistic task. The opposite is no better when the way to the baptistry is ever used while the aisle leading to spiritual maturity goes unused.

Recipe for Revolution

Acts 17:1-15

As Paul and Silas brought the gospel to Greece, the radical nature of the church became obvious. Those defending the religious status quo in Thessalonica charged that the missionaries "turned the world upside down" (KJV), were "upsetters" (Moffat), or were those that "caused trouble" (NIV). As Paul and Silas moved on to Berea, we can see a clear contrast between the satanic establishment of this world the Christian revolution which aims to free men from sin with the weapons of truth and love.

I. THE SATANIC ESTABLISHMENT ENSLAVES HUMANITY.

A. The power of this world produces closed minds. "The Jews were jealous, so they formed a mob" (v. 5).

B. The power of this world speaks with shouts for violence. "They . . . started a riot in the city . . . shouting" (vv. 5, 6).

C. The power of this world waves the flag of false patriotism. "They are defying Caesar's decrees, saying that there is another king" (v. 7).

II. THE CHRISTIAN REVOLUTION FREES HUMANITY.

A. The revolutionary gospel opens minds to listen. "They received the message with great eagerness" (v. 11).

B. The revolutionary gospel opens Bibles to evaluate claims as true or false. They "examined the Scriptures every day to see if what Paul said was true" (v. 11).

C. The revolutionary gospel opens hearts to receive truth, peace, and salvation.
"Many of the Jews believed, as did also a number of prominent Greek women and many Greek men" (v. 12).

CONCLUSION

When open to the Christian revolution, a person becomes a new creature with a new nature, a new status, and a new purpose.

TEXTUAL HIGHLIGHTS

Paul was a man of good habits. Perhaps I should say of good "customs." Let us look at a few and profit from his skill at winning others. Paul customarily went to the Jews first. Although we know him as the special apostle to the Gentiles, he never failed to start with the people of the Book. Israel had the prophecies and were looking for God's Messiah.

As was his custom, Paul searched the city for its "synagogue of the Jews." To find a place where Jehovah was named and his revelation pondered was fertile soil for the planting of the gospel. Habitually he sought to be present at the synagogue on the Sabbath days. There is no use in being in a right place at a wrong time. An empty building is not what a salesman seeks. A gathered assembly only exists at certain hours on certain days. To the Jews that day was the seventh day of the week, the Sabbath. When Paul wanted to break bread with fellow Christians, he met with them "on the first day of the week" (20:7). When his desire was to evangelize among the Jews, he entered their assembly on their holy day.

As was his custom, he used "the Scriptures." Ready and available in each synagogue would be the Torah, the Prophets, and the other Sacred Writings. Thirty-nine Spirit-inspired books existed to be searched for information regarding the Christ.

As was his custom, he "reasoned with them." Paul had a rational faith. Evidence backed his teaching. He customarily would be found "explaining and proving" from these documents what the Messiah was to do. The Old Testament affirmed he would "suffer, and rise from the dead."

Once the prophecies were heard. Paul was ready to stay with his customary plan and show Jesus to be that Christ.

ILLUSTRATION

Revolutionary faith. A small tyke argued with her sister, "I tell you, the Bible does not end in 1 Timothy; it ends in Revolutions." Toyohiko Kagawa called any Bible movement "a quiet revolution against darkness and crime."

Introducing the Unknown God

Acts 17:16-34

Americans, similar to the Athenians, have opted for many "gods" to please their every craving and passion. We need to hear the apostle's invitation to leave idolatry and meet the one true God.

I. THE TRUE GOD IS THE ALL-WISE CREATOR.

"The God who made the world and everything in it" (v. 24).

II. THE TRUE GOD IS THE OMNIPRESENT LORD.

He "is the Lord of heaven and earth and does not live in temples built by hands" (v. 24).

III. THE TRUE GOD IS THE ALL-SUFFICIENT SUSTAINER.

"He is not served by human hands, as if he needed anything, because he himself gives all men life and breath and everything else (v. 25).

IV. THE TRUE GOD IS THE ALL-LOVING FATHER.

"From one man he made every nation of men" (v. 26).
"We are his offspring" (v. 28).

V. THE TRUE GOD IS THE ALL-POWERFUL RULER.

"He determined the times set for them and the exact places where they should live" (v. 26).

VI. THE TRUE GOD IS THE ALL-RIGHTEOUS JUDGE.

"He commands all people everywhere to repent. For he has set a day when he will judge the world with justice" (vv. 30, 31).

VII. THE TRUE GOD IS THE ALL-SUFFICIENT SAVIOR.

"He will judge . . . by the man he has appointed . . . raising him from the dead" (v. 31).

CONCLUSION

Because God gave us free wills, some will "sneer" while others will want to "hear . . . again" (v. 32). From God's side, he acted "so that men would seek him and perhaps reach out for him and find him" (v. 27).

TEXTUAL HIGHLIGHTS

Paul would have made a poor travel agent. Thousands of tourists save for years and plan for months to get to see Greece. Whatever else they miss, they must return with photos of Athens. The Parthenon is a must. The ancient architecture is world-renowned. Yet, when the apostle saw it in an earlier and much better condition, he was distressed (v. 16). He did not see the art of a craftsman; he saw the superstition of idolaters. To Paul, lifestyle is affected by religion. Men below will live no better than the gods they worship. A travel agent might sell a tour to pagan temples featuring images of unclothed, frolicking gods and goddesses. Paul would seek to give light to minds darkened from following them.

Paul would have made a poor university professor of comparative religion. His personal convictions would not have allowed him to objectively hold before his students the alternate lifestyles available. He was versed in the "Epicurean and Stoic" philosophies (v. 18), but he would never degrade the faith that held him by speaking of Jesus as another of the "foreign gods" (v. 18).

Paul made an excellent preacher. He could not quiet the inner urgency to speak out for Christ. A fire burned within him. The people before him knew zero about Jehovah or his Son Jesus. They would not have recognized a Bible verse if they heard one. Yet he needed to find a way to catch their attention and guide their thoughts to Calvary and the open tomb.

The approach to use struck Paul when he saw "an altar with this inscription: TO AN UNKNOWN GOD" (v. 23). They had gods by the thousands and feared them all. Lest one be angry at being overlooked, they hoped to dupe the deity by this special niche lacking a specific name. Here was Paul's opportunity. He would introduce Jesus whom they did not know.

The Conversion of a Preacher

Acts 18:24-26

Converting people is never easy. Changing a preacher's mind may be next to impossible!

Apollos was a happy exception. Let us look at the elements of Apollos's training and background that kept his mind open and doctrine accurate.

I. THE PREACHER ALREADY HAD THE RIGHT TRAINING (v. 24).
"He was a learned man."

II. THE PREACHER ALREADY HAD THE RIGHT TEXTBOOK (v. 24).
"a thorough knowledge of the Scriptures"

III. THE PREACHER ALREADY HAD THE RIGHT CREED (v. 25).
"He taught about Jesus accurately."

IV. THE PREACHER ALREADY HAD THE RIGHT ENTHUSIASM (vv. 25, 26).
"He spoke with great fervor . . . [and did] speak boldly."

V. BUT, THE PREACHER HAD THE WRONG BAPTISM" (v. 25).
"He knew only the baptism of John."

VI. HOWEVER, THE PREACHER HAD THE RIGHT ATTITUDE (v. 26).
"Priscilla and Aquila . . . explained to him the way of God more adequately."

CONCLUSION

Congregations have couples like Priscilla and Aquilla who can add to any preacher's strength when they gently and helpfully invite their minister "to their home and explain" their suggestions.

TEXTUAL HIGHLIGHTS

Before we meet the golden-tongued Apollos, look one more time at his teachers, Priscilla and Aquila. We hear nothing but compliments concerning them in the epistles. The 1 Corinthian letter speaks of "the church that meets at their house" (16:19). This fact alone indicates their open generosity and hospitality. Paul's

Roman letter praises their sacrificial self-giving: "Greet Priscilla and Aquila, my fellow workers in Christ Jesus. They risked their lives for me" (Romans 16:3, 4). The very last epistle Paul ever wrote still calls them to mind and greets them with a "salute" (2 Timothy 4:19, KJV). With such exemplary tutors, Apollos cannot but profit. Apollos, like the twelve men spoken of in Acts 19:1-7, was a man that heard of Jesus in the days of John the Baptist. In those earlier years and in that distant land (Palestine), many heard about "Jesus accurately" (Acts 18:25). Christ's miracles were on the tongues of the populace from Galilee and beyond. Being "mighty in the scriptures" (18:24, KJV), it was not difficult for Apollos to powerfully confute the Jews, "proving from the Scriptures that Jesus was the Christ" (18:28).

Anyone seeing the evidence of Jesus' signs and examining the ancient prophecies could be made certain that he was the promised Messiah. But what if some such person moved across the miles to a distant land before that Christ's life ended in a crucifixion followed by a resurrection? Would such a person be a full-gospel preacher, or would he need the rest of the story?

The deficiency in baptism of the twelve, referred to in Acts 19, and the line of Acts 18 that Apollos knew "only the baptism of John," comes clear as we read the Synoptic Gospels. It was after his resurrection that Jesus commissioned baptism for all converts (Matthew 28:19).

ILLUSTRATION

Some today only want a preacher who has either a Master's degree or a Doctorate. Dwight L. Moody believed one must have two degrees: a B.A. and an O.O.—that is he must be Born Again and Out and Out!

Correcting Deficient Teaching

Acts 19:1-7

In Acts 18 we learn that Apollos was a gifted teacher who did not have complete knowledge of his subject matter. Priscilla and Aquila corrected one part of the problem by tactfully supplementing his education.

Yet another complication existed. What about those who came to faith in Jesus through the teaching of Apollos? Luke tells us the steps Paul took to correct deficiencies in Bible teaching.

I. PAUL DETERMINED THE EXTENT OF THE PROBLEM (vv. 1, 2).

A. The question: "Did you receive the Holy Spirit when you believed?" Believers in Jesus during his earthly ministry were instructed by his presence. The Spirit was given to lead believers into truth during the age of the church.

B. The response: "No, we have not even heard that there is a Holy Spirit." The problem was obviously of a great enough extent that it required Paul to intervene. In this case, deficient teaching caused a tremendous void in the lives of those who would follow Jesus.

II. PAUL DETERMINED THE REASON FOR THE PROBLEM (vv. 3, 4).

A. The question: "What baptism did you receive?" Paul's inquiry was aimed at learning if they had come to Jesus after Christ's passion or prior to it. "Up to that time the Spirit had not been given, since Jesus had not yet been glorified" (John 7:39). Before the outpouring of the Spirit in Acts 2, the Spirit's abiding presence in men was but a promise. After that Pentecostal founding of the kingdom, the Holy Spirit abides in the church.

B. The response: "John's baptism." This response told Paul what he needed to know. An important part of their education had been omitted.

III. PAUL TOOK ACTION TO ADDRESS THE PROBLEM (vv. 5-7).

A. Paul rebaptized these men after they recognized that their theology was deficient.

B. After Paul laid his hands on them, "the Holy Spirit came on them, and they spoke in tongues and prophesied." Note the similarity between Acts 2, Acts 10, and this event.

ILLUSTRATION

Should I be baptized again? This unusual case study that Luke presents to us may cause one to consider whether or not he or she needs to take some strong action to reaffirm his or her faith. The rebaptism of these twelve men has caused some to ask whether or not they should be rebaptized.

In this case, the men had been baptized in recognition of their sinfulness, as John had commanded. They had not been baptized to reenact the death, burial, and resurrection of Jesus in their own lives (Romans 6:4), declaring themselves dead to sin and accepting a new life through the empowering Spirit (Acts 2:38). Their first baptism was essentially different from Christian baptism.

When one submits to Christian baptism and later understands the act more fully or develops a deeper sense of commitment to Jesus, rebaptism is no more necessary than would be remarriage when one more fully understands that partnership or develops a deeper sense of commitment to his or her spouse. Likewise, rebaptism after each time one sins betrays a misunderstanding of the once-for-all work of Christ (as well as potentially contributing to pneumonia!). Perceived ritualistic deficiencies in an original baptism such as location, credentials of the baptizer, or words spoken at the time also miss the point that the power in baptism is divine, not human.

The men in Acts 19 were baptized again because their first baptism was not Christian baptism. It appears that the only reason for another baptism is that if the first was not Christian baptism, the immersion of a repentant adult believer wishing to begin life anew by the power of God's Spirit.

The Danger of Sleeping in Church

Acts 20:1-12

On their way to Jerusalem, the missionary team stopped in the city of Troas. In relating the story of that stay, Luke includes a strangely amusing anecdote. As Paul preached a long sermon in a crowded and stuffy room, a young man named Eutychus fell asleep and fell out of an upstairs window! Tragedy was turned to celebration as Eutychus was raised back to life.

It is pardonable and sometimes understandable that one would physically fall asleep in church. A much bigger danger, however, exists when one forgets why the church assembles in the first place and becomes spiritually lethargic. In the story of Eutychus we see some distinctives of worship concerning which he and the early church were alert.

I. EUTYCHUS WAS NOT ASLEEP CONCERNING THE LORD'S TREASURY (vv. 1-5).

A. Paul was gathering funds for the poor in Jerusalem (Galatians 2:10).

B. Paul's purpose was to demonstrate the unity of the church (2 Corinthians 8:1-15).

C. Paul's desire was to have area representatives responsible for safe delivery "Berea . . . Thessalonica . . . Derbe . . . Asia" (Acts 20:4).

II. EUTYCHUS WAS NOT ASLEEP CONCERNING THE LORD' S DAY (vv. 6, 7)

A. The church did not come together Monday through Saturday. "We stayed seven days."

B. The church assembled on Sunday. "On the first day of the week we came together." (See Hebrews 10:25.)

III. EUTYCHUS WAS NOT ASLEEP CONCERNING THE LORD'S SUPPER (v. 7)

A. This one Sunday the congregation heard from Paul.

B. Every Sunday the congregation communed with Christ. "We came together to break bread."

TEXTUAL HIGHLIGHTS

Paul and his many companions from across his mission fields were to spend seven days in Troas (Acts 20:6). He was anxious that the funds gathered from Gentile churches reach the needy brethren in Jerusalem. He would book no delays to be in that city "by the day of Pentecost" (20:16). At such a Jewish feast, many people would be gathered together. There the contributed money might reach the brethren in need. The reason for the seven-day stay, in the midst of a nonstop flight to the holy city, seems to be the coveted opportunity to be with the gathered church at its "first day of the week" assembly (20:7).

As a missionary, Paul customarily was to be found in Jewish synagogues on the Sabbath. Then his purpose was to lead non-Christians (but potential believers) into the church. In Acts 20 his goal is otherwise. His aim has become to gather together in worship with those of like precious faith. Luke states the purpose of the "first day of the week" meeting in these words: "we came together to break bread" (20:7). While the occasion gave Paul opportunity to discourse with the people, the goal of the assembly was "to break bread."

Just as in Acts 2:42, the "breaking of bread" is associated with other acts of worship. Thus Acts 20:7 is a significant glimpse into the type of worship service practiced in early times.

Believers in Jesus assembled around a table. There, in communion with their risen Savior, they did "proclaim the Lord's death." This they vowed to do "until he comes" (1 Corinthians 11: 26). Whatever similarity there accidentally may be in the worship of Jews, Moslems, and other theists, the church of Jesus Christ alone observes the distinctive practice of the Lord's Supper. Ancient records from across the Roman world show Communion to be the heart of Lord's day praise.

ILLUSTRATION

Sleeping in church. It has been said, "If all the people who fall to sleep during a sermon were laid end-to-end, they would be more comfortable."

His Task Before Us, His Power Behind Us

Acts 20:17-35

The book of Acts contains several sample sermons. Yet only one of those sermons is addressed to Christian workers. When Paul spoke to the Ephesian elders on the island of Miletus, he gave insight useful to every Christian worker today.

I. CHRISTIAN WORKERS HAVE GOD' S THREE-FOLD ASSIGNMENT (vv. 28-31).

A. Watch out for your own spiritual welfare (v. 28). "Guard yourselves." Followers cannot rise above the standards set by their leaders.

B. Watch out for your sheep (v. 28). "Keep watch over . . . all the flock of which the Holy Spirit has made you overseers." We must protect those with whose welfare we have been entrusted.

C. Watch out for the wolves (vv. 29-31). "Savage wolves will come in among you and will not spare the flock." Take your opposition seriously.

II. CHRISTIAN WORKERS HAVE GOD'S THREE-FOLD ASSISTANCE (vv. 32-35).

A. His presence is near, so trust and pray (v. 32). "Now I commit you to God." As God's servants we are under both his care and his command. We must pray, seeking both direction and support.

B. His gospel is clear, so learn and teach (v. 32). "Now I commit you . . . to the word of his grace." We have the clear, written Word of God, the source of all we need to learn for success in life and the source for all that we teach others.

C. His task is here, so help (vv. 34, 35). "These hands of mine have supplied my own needs and the needs of my companions." Hard work blesses ourselves and others.

CONCLUSION

The great blessing that is ours in receiving Christ is even overshadowed by the blessing of sharing him.

TEXTUAL HIGHLIGHTS

Thanks Luke! Were it not for your recording Paul's sermon to the Ephesian elders, we would never have known Jesus' words about giving. None of our Gospels preserve this important sentence uttered by our Lord: "It is more blessed to give than to receive" (Acts 20:35). How many times have we recalled the instruction when opportunities to share financially have confronted us? A mission needs help. The hungry cry of an impoverished child needing to be fed. Another unit of building must go up so more children can be reached with the Christian message. These will be blessed in receiving. But how much more blessed are we in the giving!

I suggest teachers and preachers not overlook how applicable this saying is in their ministries. There is no question that those in the classrooms, or the pews, are blessed under these ministries of the Word. But I do not need to tell any servant of that Word what a blessing it is to give forth the message of truth. Note in our passage what a giver Paul was to Ephesus.

He taught "night and day" (20:31). To do that required giving up a lot of other activities. He could have limited his efforts to the light hours. He might have stopped after a few modest hours of effort.

Paul did this all-out teaching "for three years" without ceasing (20:31). "What a benefit to the people of Asia," we might say. "What a blessing to me," Paul might add. "It is more blessed to give than to receive."

The text says more than "three years." It speaks of more than "night and day." It adds the words "with tears." That is the kind of preaching that costs the speaker something. Being burdened about people's souls is emotionally draining but highly rewarding to listener and message-bearer.

ILLUSTRATION

Read the instructions. A list of instructions accompanies products that require assembly by the purchaser. That is true of complicated toys, farming equipment, or office computers. After hours of do-it-yourself struggle the advice comes to mind: "When all else fails, read the instructions." That goes for building lives for Christ as well.

Testimony Time

Acts 22:1-22

There is value in personal testimony. God works in the lives of his people. We can rejoice as we hear what he has done. Yet there is special value in apostolic testimony. When the apostle Paul stops to tell about God's work in his life, we know we can learn great truth.

I. PAUL GIVES ACCOUNT OF HIMSELF B.C., BEFORE CONVERSION (vv. 3-5).

A. He tells of his birth (v. 3). "I am a Jew, born in Tarsus of Cilicia."

B. He tells of his education (v. 3). "Under Gamaliel I was thoroughly trained in the law."

C. He tells of his zeal (v. 3). "[I am] just as zealous for God as any of you are today."

D. He tells of his persecution (vv. 4, 5, 19, 20). "I persecuted the followers of this Way to their death."

II. PAUL GIVES ACCOUNT OF HIMSELF A.C., AT CONVERSION (vv. 6-16).

A. He meets Jesus, enabling him to become an apostle (vv. 6-15). "You will be his witness to all men of what you have seen."

B. He meets Jesus' conditions, enabling him to become a Christian (v. 16). "What are you waiting for? Get up, be baptized."

III. PAUL GIVES ACCOUNT OF HIMSELF A.D., AFTER DELIVERANCE (vv. 17-22).

A. When God speaks, the willing start serving (v. 21). "Go; I will send you far away to the Gentiles."

B. When God speaks, the unwilling stop listening (v. 22). "The crowd listened until he said this."

TEXTUAL HIGHLIGHTS

What a difference language makes. There can be no communication without it. There may be little interest in trying to grasp what another is attempting to say, if that person has not paid the price of learning to speak the language of the hearer. On the mission field the very fact that a "foreign" Christian cared enough to learn another culture, another lifestyle, and another tongue has served to open ears to hearing what that person came so far to say.

Look at Paul. The interest of the chief captain peaked the moment he heard Paul speak fluent Greek. Prior to that he thought him to be an "Egyptian" leader of insurrection (Acts 21:37, 38). "Do you speak Greek?" was the question that marked the reversal of his attitude toward his prisoner. Similarly the Jewish mob was filled with hatred toward Paul and sought his death. What can the apostle do to open their minds so that gospel seed can be sown there? Paul spoke to them in "Aramaic" (21:40). That made the difference. That brought a hush. Soon after the speech drew toward its conclusion, the silence was interrupted by shouts calling for his death (22:22). However, the word had been preached. The key that unlocked the opportunity was the use of the listener's language. "When they heard him speak to them in Aramaic, they became very quiet" (22:2).

ILLUSTRATION

Life-saving listening. Where a railway track intersects a heavily traveled road there is a warning sign calling for our attention. If there are no flashing lights or clanging bells, there is at least the clearly lettered sign with the words, "stop, look, and listen." Woe to the traveler on life's road that doesn't stop long enough to carefully, look both directions (into his past and forward to his future). This is the time to listen with both ears, for failing to listen can cost a life.

Faith on Trial

Acts 24:1-21

It is not unusual for Christians today to meet harsh criticism. In a day when cynicism and moral ambiguity are the norm, those who stand for absolute truth may come under attack. We may be called "naive," "narrow," or even "intolerant" in a world that refuses to hear our message.

This is nothing new. In Acts 24 Paul was called to defend his faith in a hostile world. When even some of the Jews were known for their doubt (28:8), Paul was accused of being a "troublemaker" and the leader of a divisive "sect" (24:5). Paul's response at that time is equally relevant today.

I. WE HAVE FAITH IN ALL THE BIBLE. THAT IS NOT NAIVE! (v. 14).

A. Paul argued that his faith had both roots in history and in a written document that had long been accepted as authoritative.

1. "I worship the God of our fathers."
2. "I believe everything that agrees with the Law and . . . Prophets."

B. There have been doubters in every age, but the Word of God has withstood every attack. The Bible continues to provide reliable direction and credible answers to those willing to seek.

II. WE HAVE HOPE FOR ALL THE DEAD. THAT IS NOT NARROW! (vv. 15, 16).

A. "I have the same hope in God . . . that there will be a resurrection."

B. Christ arose to approve his deity.

1. The righteous will arise to share Heaven's joys.
2. The wicked will arise to receive their judgment.

C. A belief in God's justice should cause believers today, like Paul, to strive to live with integrity "before God and man."

III. WE HAVE LOVE FOR ALL THE PEOPLE. THAT IS NOT HATEFUL! (v. 17).

A. "I came to bring my people gifts for the poor."

B. The apostle to the Gentiles brought money for the poor Jews.

C. The love of God should be obvious in the church's love for others yet today.

TEXTUAL HIGHLIGHTS

When the lawyer Tertullus sought to prejudice Felix against the apostle, he used the pejorative: "a ringleader of the Nazarene sect" (Acts 24:5). Nazareth was a despised town. It was common opinion that nothing good could come from such a lowly community as that where Jesus was reared. Tie Paul to the town of disrepute and tar him with the brash "troublemaker" and the seed of distrust will be planted.

Paul cites clear facts that persuasively point otherwise. He "went up to Jerusalem to worship" (24:11). Witnesses saw him in three places. He did go to the "temple." He was to be seen in various synagogues." No one would deny he was in "the city." But worshiper he was, not troublemaker.

The hatred against Christ's spokesman, however, was religiously based. The conflict, at bottom, was belief versus unbelief. Religious titles cannot hide rejection of Scriptural teaching in mind and heart. If you ask how much of the Old Testament Bible was authoritative to a Sadducee, his creed would give answer, "no resurrection, and that there are neither angels, nor spirits" (23:8). But inquire of the Christian preacher and he tells of believing "everything that agrees with the Law and that is written in the Prophets" (24:14). Law and Prophets is one way of referring to every part of the Bible from first book to last. Some may be skeptical of certain Old Testament stories, or raise doubts regarding some Bible penmen, but not the followers of Jesus. Christ showed insights from the sacred pages that left his disciples firm in their confidence about the revelation from God. Once the case for the Scriptures was made, belief in "the resurrection" was near (24:21).

Delightful Delusions

Acts 24:24-27

We can be entertained when we allow ourselves to be fooled. We may watch an illusionist perform a feat we know to be impossible, but allow our amazement to overcome our skepticism. We watch a film or TV program about fictional people in improbable situations. We react with enjoyment rather than scorn because, when it comes to entertainment, we have the ability to suspend our disbelief.

When it comes to the serious business of God and faith, we dare not deceive ourselves, however. The story of Paul and Felix illustrates some delightful delusions we must avoid when it comes to salvation.

I. IT IS A DELUSION TO THINK THAT A CHURCH CONNECTION ASSURES FINANCIAL GAIN (v. 26).

A. "He [Felix] was hoping that Paul would offer him a bribe."

B. Some join a church thinking it offers business contacts, political influence, social prestige. Such expectations will never be fully met.

II. IT IS A DELUSION TO THINK THAT PLEASING MEN WILL BRING SECURITY (v. 27).

A. "Because Felix wanted to grant a favor to the Jews, he left Paul in prison."

B. One seeking the popularity of the world may lose his popularity with the Lord. The applause of men is not as important as Christ's words "Well done!"

III. IT IS A DELUSION TO THINK THAT FEAR IS A LEGITIMATE REASON TO AVOID MAKING A DECISION (v. 25).

A. "As Paul discoursed on righteousness, self-control and the judgment to come, Felix was afraid."

B. Coming face to face with an awesome God is frightening. Ignoring him, however, will not make truth go away.

IV. IT IS A DELUSION TO THINK CONVERSION WILL EVER BE CONVENIENT (v. 25).

A. "When I find it convenient, I will send for you."

B. The hardest step in the "steps of salvation" is repentance. Facing up to wrongs done and breaking from old habits demands courage and decisive choice.

TEXTUAL HIGHLIGHTS

Felix should have known that you can't get blood out of a turnip nor a bribe out of a preacher. But he tried. And he tried some more.

The evil thought was placed in Felix's mind by the tempter. Most of the early evangelists were men of meager existence, but Paul was in a different situation. He had promoted large and generous offerings from Gentile churches for Jewish brethren. This try for manifesting church oneness captured Paul's imagination. Month after month, letter after letter, visit after visit encouraged many churches to pitch in. The funds gathered from across the mission fields and transported by special messengers had been brought to Jerusalem where Paul's capture began. Felix believed that if he detained Paul's release, this man would grow tired of detainment. With Paul's many friends and exceptional know-how, he could raise any money needed. Will not loss of freedom, plus access to funds, equal Felix's desired bribe? The one factor missing in the equation was Paul's Christian character. Luke records that in two years "Felix was succeeded by Porcius Festus" (24:27). But nowhere can it be written Felix "succeeded."

We wish the apostle could have been successful in reaching Felix for God. "He reasoned" (24:25, KJV) with a man who was not reasonable. He preached "righteousness" to one who lived in wickedness. He spoke of "self-control" to a leader who had lost all control. He announced "judgment" to a person that would bury his head in sand rather than face the reality of a coming accounting. Paul didn't get the response of conversion that he hoped for, but he got an applause of a kind. The governor's knees applauded. "Felix was afraid" (24:25). He could have been justified.

Where Witnessing Is Appropriate

Acts 26:17, 18

Where are the witnesses of Christ's power called to testify? As Paul was on trial before Agrippa, he recounts his commission to rescue the Gentiles with his testimony of Jesus. Though his witness eventually led him to be tried before the high Roman official of the region, Paul never backed down. As we review the events of the book of Acts to this point, we see a great variety of situations in which believers were similarly faithful to their commission.

I. **IN ACTS 2 WE SEE JESUS PREACHED ON THE STREET CORNER.**
"Those who accepted his message were . . . about three thousand" (2:41).

II. **IN ACTS 3 WE SEE JESUS PREACHED ON THE CHURCH STEPS.**
"All the people were astonished and came running to them in the place called Solomon's Colonnade" (3:11).

III. **IN ACTS 8 WE SEE JESUS PREACHED ON A MOVING BUS.**
"Then Philip ran up to the chariot . . . [the eunuch] invited Philip to . . . sit with him" (8:30, 31).

IV. **IN ACTS 16 WE SEE JESUS PREACHED ON THE BEACH AND IN THE JAIL.**
"On the Sabbath we went outside the city gate to the river" (16:13).
"The jailer woke up, and saw the prison doors open" (16:27).

V. **IN ACTS 17 WE SEE JESUS PREACHED IN THE MARKETPLACE.**
"He reasoned in the synagogue . . . as well as in the marketplace" (17:17).

VI. **IN ACTS 25 WE SEE JESUS PREACHED IN THE GOVERNMENT HALLS.**
"Agrippa and Bernice . . . entered the audience room with the high ranking officers and the leading men of the city" (25:23).

TEXTUAL HIGHLIGHTS

Why preach? What is the purpose of heralding the news of Christ? Is the consequence of gospel proclamation worth the effort? The answer is found in words spoken to Paul on the road to Damascus. Jesus gives to the former persecutor, Saul of Tarsus, the privilege of becoming the herald of Christian truth. The apostle will later address letters as from "Paul, called to be an apostle of Christ Jesus by the will of God" (1 Corinthians 1:1). Now, at his commissioning he hears the divine voice order, "Now get up and stand on your feet. I have appeared to you to appoint you as a servant and as a witness of what you have seen of me and what I will show you" (Acts 26:16). But what will be the result of such news-sharing? That is the important question to those who continue spreading the story.

Preaching turns hearers "from darkness to light" (26:18). Ignorance is dispelled by revelation. Truth overcomes superstition. Proclamation delivers enslaved minds "from the power of Satan to God." Some power will control man. God's might from above is offered as the alternate to evil power from below.

Heralding the story of the cross and resurrection offers "forgiveness of sins" in the place of condemnation because of sins. A guilty conscience can be replaced by a cleansed conscience. Only hearing God's gracious message can bring that release.

God's proclaimed word offers an inheritance of God's glory to man. So many people feel that life has passed them by. They have nothing. They belong to no one. Hearing the church's announcement changes all that. Someone died and left them a fortune. It was Jesus. Now, in him, they are somebody and they belong to everybody in God's family. Today the once outcasts are "sanctified by faith" in Christ (26:18).

ILLUSTRATION

Where do I serve him? A young man asked for direction on finding a place of service for Christ. "What shall I do for Christ?" was his question. "Go where he is not, and take him with you," was the response of the white-haired minister.

The Fine Art of Becoming a Christian

Acts 26:27-29

What an unusual court hearing! Paul ends his testimony before Agrippa with an invitation! In these few verses we see how desperately God desires men and women to be saved.

I. GOD WANTS MEN CONVERTED WITHOUT A HESITATION (v. 28).

"Do you think that in such a short time you can persuade me to be a Christian?"

A. There is no reason to delay: What more could God do, promise, or prove?

B. There is great danger in delay: A human may lose life, interest, or opportunity.

C. There is Satanic deception in delay: He offers another way and/or another time.

II. GOD WANTS MEN CONVERTED WITHOUT A RESERVATION (v. 29).

"Short time or long—I pray God that . . . you . . . may become what I am."

A. God wants time from busy people.

B. God wants money from able people.

C. God wants talents from capable people.

III. GOD WANTS MEN CONVERTED WITHOUT AN EXCEPTION (v. 29).

"Not only you but all who are listening to me today"

A. Heaven has room for sinners, like Paul.

B. Heaven has room for sinners, like Agrippa.

C. Heaven has room for sinners, like me.

CONCLUSION

You are invited to be a Christian quickly, completely, and unanimously!

TEXTUAL HIGHLIGHTS

Happiness is a warm puppy to Charlie Brown and his friends of the comic strips. Happiness is an opportunity to preach Christ. Paul stands before Herod Agrippa as a prisoner. Yet he utters in all honesty the opening line, "King Agrippa, I consider myself fortunate to stand before you today as I make my defense against all the accusations of the Jews" (Acts 26:2).

It was a Herod that sought to destroy Jesus as a baby (Matthew 2:13). It was one in the Herod line that ordered God's prophet, John the Baptist, to be beheaded. That Herod was a tetrarch after the death of his father. Now Paul has a chance to reach out with the gospel toward another horrid Herod—Herod Agrippa II. From the beginning of the Christian story the anti-Christs included all that family that flowed from the loins of Herod the Great.

Can such reprobates be redeemed? Are violent enemies of the cross apt to become heralds of the Calvary event? In other words, is the gospel "the power of God for the salvation of everyone" (Romans 1:16), or only to the few who have but waded around the edges of the pool of iniquity? No one was more convinced of the transforming power of the gospel than the tentmaker standing before Agrippa. He would later write, "A trustworthy saying that deserves full acceptance: Christ Jesus came into the world to save sinners—of whom I am the worst" (1 Timothy 1:15). Had Paul's message been preceded by a modern solo, it would have been likely "It Is No Secret (What God Can Do)." The gospel worked, works, and will continue to work life transformation. Paul did "pray God" that he could persuade the king to be a "Christian" (Acts 26:28, 29).

Smooth Sailing Over Rough Waters

Acts 27:13–28:10

Life is like a sea voyage. There will be pleasant days and "quiet waters" (Psalm 23:2), but there are apt to be times of frightening storms. By looking at the literal storm Paul survived in Acts 27, we can find principles for overcoming the figurative storms confronting us.

I. UNDERSTAND THERE MAY BE CALM BEFORE THE STORM, BUT ROUGH DAYS ARE CERTAIN TO COME (vv. 13, 14).

A. "A gentle south wind began to blow. . . . Before very long, a wind of hurricane force, called the 'northeaster,' swept down from the island."

B. Rough storms may blow into our nation, our congregation, and into our lives.

II. UNDERSTAND THERE CAN BE CALM DURING THE STORM, FOR GOD'S ASSISTANCE WILL COME (vv. 20- 22).

A. "We finally gave up all hope of being saved. . . . [Paul said] "I urge you to keep up your courage, because not one of you will be lost."

B. God is a God of providence as well as a God of promise (Romans 8:28).

III. UNDERSTAND THERE WILL BE CALM AFTER THE STORM, SINCE OPPORTUNITIES TO MINISTER WILL COME.

A. You can minister to people who heard you pray (27:35).
"He took some bread and gave thanks to God in front of them."

B. You can minister to people who saw you help (28:3).
"Paul gathered a pile of brushwood and . . . put it on the fire."

TEXTUAL HIGHLIGHTS

No one but an eyewitness could have written the thrilling saga of Acts 27 and 28. The dangerous voyage, the frightening shipwreck, and the total rescue of life was experienced by Luke before it was penned by him. From the "we" of the first verse to the "we" of the next and final chapter, the reader relives the exciting sea journey that brought Paul toward Rome.

In the first leg of the journey, Paul is but one of a number of prisoners under the centurion's charge. At the end of the account the apostle is on the center of the stage with all eyes glued toward him. The providential hand of God is seen in between. It works the circumstances so that his spokesman can move from obscurity to the focus of attention. It is not important that Paul be seen only as just another prisoner. But it is vital that his message of Christ be heard. Otherwise life will shipwreck one day for all of them. Down will go their hopes. To the bottom will go their dreams. Into unfathomable depths of degradation and despair will life itself sink without a Saviour.

If you will forgive allegorizing Scripture this one time, all men need cast "four anchors" (27:29) in the storms of life. They will do well to anchor in God's love. That is immovable. They also should cast anchor in God's promises, his Son, and his church.

ILLUSTRATIONS

Using your religion. A North Carolina preacher, B. J. Howard, had a man bemoan all the problems that came upon him in the last year. The parishioner added, "It's enough to make a man lose his religion!" The minister quietly replied, "It seems it is enough to make a man use his religion."

We have an anchor. Priscilla J. Owen's hymn "We Have an Anchor" raises the important question in the verse: "Will your anchor hold in the storms of life, When the clouds unfold their wings of strife?" The chorus sings out the Christian's answer: "We have an anchor that keeps the soul Steadfast and sure while the billows roll."